The
KINGDOMS
of
MY HEART

JOHN SADLER

ISBN 978-1-0980-5976-7 (paperback)
ISBN 978-1-0980-5977-4 (digital)

Christian Faith Publishing, Inc.
832 Park Avenue
Meadville, PA 16335
www.christianfaithpublishing.com

Printed in the United States of America

Contents

Introduction

"The Kingdoms of My Heart" is similar to my first book, "Come Let Us Adore Him." It's similar in that it takes you here, there, and everywhere in the topics that are covered. That is sort of where life takes us and that's where Jesus is waiting to lead and guide us all along the way. Know that He is right beside you and waiting for you to let Him in.

The Kingdoms of My Heart
(Luke 17:21)

When having thoughts not aligned with Christ
I would too often inwardly pray
Jesus be the kingdoms of my heart
Give me a renewal and a brand new start

As time went on those prayers faded
Jesus is becoming the kingdoms of my heart
His desire is our whole hearts to belong to Him
What do we do to make room and let Him in

We have a number of our heart chambers
In need of our attention and cleaning out
To remove the worldly things of our attention
To make room for heavenly treasures for retention

The Pharisees asked when the kingdom would come
Jesus said, "God's kingdom is not what can be seen
God's kingdom is a kingdom within you
His spirit will lead in what you need"

To raise and praise the name of Jesus
Among the many that are most desperate
To release the bonds that hold them prisoner
By God's grace we have a new family member

God's kingdom grows as hearts are won for Him
His Spirit has forever changed and molded our within
We are walking kingdoms of Jesus Christ our King
To be bringers of who Jesus wants us to bring

When we are gone Christ will have appointed
A new set of believer bringers anointed
To show his love for them to be born again
His kingdom will continue and have no end

From one saint to another to another
We leave for our heavenly kingdom realm
What glories of heaven will be revealed
Our wish list to the Father, Son, and Spirit filled

These gifts will be our everyday experiences
One or two on earth would be earth-shattering to us
But in heaven His glories will be our daily bread
It's God's way of nurturing us and our being fed

There's no limit to how many Christ wants
Can He handle and take care of the many
Remember the multitudes He fed in two ways
Bodies were fed and spirits were wed

His promises have sealed our forever with Christ
Our heavenly Father will welcome us in
And a heavenly fuss will be made over us
By God's angels with their joyful grins

Joyful is the man who puts His trust in Christ
For out of Him rivers of living water will flow
To water the fields ripe unto harvest
That the harvest for Jesus will grow

Jesus to us let Your kingdom come
Into our hearts as it is in heaven
For by the Father's love you were given
All your blessings we receive are love driven

The kingdoms of our hearts have become the kingdom of
    our God
Thanks be to our loving Lord we are included
And He is closer to us than we can assess
Thank You Lord we can leave this earthly mess

To go to the place You have prepared for us
The heavenly mansion that will be our forever home
To learn of You and know of You
Our time on earth with Christ well spent

This Organized Mess

From before the time of man began
God knew He would send His Son with His plan
To redeem and reorganize the mess of man
And to adopt us

What a messy part of His creation we are
Of all His creatures He gave us a will to choose
To reject the bad so we wouldn't lose
To the enemy of our souls

God gave us His Word from long ago
His commandments to structure our lives
he loved us so much for His Son to come
Coming so our dead bodies would be revived

From dust we came and to dust we will go
What can be in between this time frame
Jesus in His teaching wants us to know
Is victory for those who follow Him

Jesus has set a path for us to follow
With His presence in His Word we read
The Word became flesh and dwelt among us
For us to know He's the Savior we need

There's no other way to contain this mess
Than by the leading of our God and King
To cast all our cares upon Him
Jesus accepts all the cares that we bring

A spot in Heaven with our King
With the Good Shepherd to take us in
In His fold as wayward sheep
My what a mess we have been

He takes us on to live with Him
What a messy work lies ahead
To rid us of all the pitfalls
Of sin that causes us to stall

As time goes on the messiness clears
When we give our lives and hearts to Him
To clear the way for our King
To reach us all the way to where we are

This removed and that thrown out
Of the things that made us who we were
How did we even treasure this trash
Keeping us from seeing God's true path

How pure and unencumbered
The path that leads us to our King
He's waiting with arms opened wide
To receive us in Heaven, for a long, long while

We're the Us in Jesus

We're the *us* in Jesus
He's called on us to play our part
Praise God He's opened up the doors
Don't wait too long to get your start

There's nothing you have done He can't forgive
He loves you as much as any other
His time on the cross was the time you needed
To become an us in Jesus and a brother

There's so many connections He wants to make
Using all the connections of His us's
Our Jesus has put everything in order
To send His chosen to cross our border

We're the us's of Jesus Christ our King
Showing us the fields white unto harvest
Everywhere and everyone we see
Can see Jesus as beautiful, amazing and marvelous

When it's time for your sins to be forgiven
The total will come out to be zero
Because you've become an us with us
And made Jesus your eternal hero

When you give your life to Jesus
You've been deeded for all eternity
Registered in His great courthouse
As an us in Jesus's family

It's not too late and not too soon
To become an us with all of us
For Jesus is coming back to claim
All His us's that mean so much

It's a miracle we've become an us to Him
He's had His eyes on us from in the past
To nurture and make something beautiful
A jewel whose brilliance will forever last

He calls us friend and we're a friend indeed
Jesus showing what a friend can really mean
For He's made His choice for us to be
Something beautiful for the world to see

So let us come and adore our King
He came to draw us ever closer to Him
And sent us forth for others to bring
To know what our Father by the Son has done

The Wanda Effect

A poem for Wanda Campbell, the wife of Jack Campbell,
my high school football coach

When you come into the influence
Of one who stands out for Christ
Who has been a great example
Of a wife to husband sacrifice

The caregiver of all caregivers
Her love has kept her by his side
Jesus her example trying to perfect
And with her love has formed the Wanda Effect

The Wanda Effect is something special
For all wives and mothers to emulate
A light so bright for her family
She's a beacon for the many

She has a blessed commitment
To stay beside her mate
In life things happen hard to contemplate
But the Wanda Effect has been effective

What she's done for John
Long ago was begun
To secure their ties with each other
What a blessing going through life together

Many years have come and gone
Going through life's tough choices
She's been faithful without dismay
The Wanda Effect has had its way

It has been a great experience
To see the Wanda Effect at work
She stands out as a faithful wife
In order to show how life can work

As for me and many others
We stand back and take it in
We're better off for knowing her
The Wanda Effect has affected our within

A win in life with a cost and a price
It wasn't too much for her to wager
She's been uplifted and taken care of
By Jesus her blessed Savior

For the many men her husband did influence
Influence for life to make right choices
We know behind every good man
Is a good woman to set their courses

This is a note to a godly woman
Wanda we're thankful for your life
And the course that you have chosen
Your life's lessons into us have been woven

You are the perfect example
Of how a wife should be
We of the outside the family crowd
Wish for your kind of wife-ing for us

Missed the Boat

One wonders have they missed the boat
When it comes to a trip to glory
Sometimes going slow and sometimes fast
At a point in time leaving behind the past

The Father and the Son have equipped the boat
To be a welcoming vessel to all
No matter what your stature, be it short or be it tall
Be it round or be it thin all are welcomed in

God can control His vessel's speed
To slow down just for you
He doesn't want a stranger
To miss out on what He has for you

To become equipped and a child of God
See wonders up close and afar
The work that His saints are doing
Is the work that keeps them going

Jesus is the captain to steer the boat
The boat to heaven it is going
At arrival it's time to depart
Another wharf load waiting for their start

The start of loading and getting there
Embarking at His time He's given
Our passports are paid for and in order
His angels welcoming across heaven's border

If heaven's doors have opened for you
You're on the boat you've never missed
There's a boat moored and waiting
Those reluctant to come and be Christ's guests

Christ has done all that's needed for all
To have a chance to receive His call
Calling all to repent and get on board
His love boat that can hold us all

If you're afraid you've missed the boat
It's right for you to be afraid
Fear of the Lord is the beginning of wisdom
It's time to be added to His kingdom

Off the Hook

Off the hook is giving you a reprieve
You can breathe a little easier now
What you were worrying about has gone away
Being on the hook may be coming for another day

But for now your life seems to be right
Everything is going just great for you
Just great is using the world's definition
Of what you've accomplished just for you

Just for you and not for the anybodies
To where the world is so lacking of
Someone to step up and help the ones
So desperately seeking help from the anyones

You can be an anyone God can rely on
To spread His love and help all over
You'll feel a growing appreciation
God's presence in your life forever

Being off the hook for your sins
Jesus loved you and took you in
He went on the hook of the cross
The nails being the hook was the cost

The suffering and the pain were part of it
That our Jesus endured for you
The separation from His Father most hurtful
The Father-Son relationship took a hit

Jesus had never been separated
From His Father from the beginning of time
At the cross He felt the awful anguish
And at the cross your sins relinquished

In the Barn

Christ's relationship to us has done one thing
Our souls for eternity are in the barn
The miracle is amazing and humbling for sure
Every day growing in Christ more and more

There was a time of eternal choosing
We'd make the right choice instead of losing
The gifts He gave for us to use
Being in the barn was of His choosing

Christ chose us all from long ago
To be His barn help to help others
His word and spirit are always reinforcing
In His presence we are eternally rejoicing

Rejoicing that He's placed us in the barn
In the barn of His protection and wooing
He's wooed for us to be for sure
None He's wooed He would be losing

How good does it feel to be in the barn
And lovingly and caringly bedded down
All we need is provided to nurture
our spiritual health and all our future

There will be a barn full we will see
Because God's children have been fruitful
To bring the lost and hurting ones
To the barn and to Him most grateful

Flying Blind

When we are born and growing up
Testing our wings, off to the wild blue yonder
Guided by our parents and those around us
The world noticing and pause to ponder

Much more than the world's noticing
is the Father, Son, and Spirit's attention
Their intention for their pilots
is to fly right for them

Without the guiding of Who cares the most
we're off on the wrong flight path
Sooner or later we will find
We lifted off in the world flying blind

Flying blind can't help our navigation
To get to the place of God's intention
God's wisdom will steer us to Him
If we acknowledge Him for who He is

When you take off to get somewhere
You have in mind where you'll be landing
Don't let some wind blow you off course
Your navigator will keep you in good standing

Christ is the master navigator
mastering all the ifs, ands, the buts
His word and spirit is the flight plan
For us to take off and not to crash

The Best of Me

Who deserves the best of me
It's Jesus from the Father given
He came to give the best of Himself
It's time to come down from the forgotten shelf

The forgotten shelf is a place not to be
How can you bring the best of you
If you're put away and not on display
So dust yourself off and get in someone's way

Christ came to get in the way of Satan
He intervened to show us the way
"The Way" was the first name for Christians
That's who I've become, I praise that day

We all have been dealt a winning hand
The Father the dealer and we the winner
If we play our hand just right
We will come out as the givers

Christ in His word has given the victory
To all who will obey and serve
We couldn't be givers except for Christ
Giving the best of us is what He deserves

Be careful you protect the best of you
It is precious and why Jesus came
To claim the pot of the winnings
For us to all give honor to His name

Christ gave His best and it was enough
To capture the best of our whole hearts
So give the best of you to Him
Jesus will help you to be all in

All in for what His sacrifice means
For the world to be amazed
He meant to claim as many
His desire is to not lose any

The Father sees that the best of you
Has been won for His purposes
To proclaim the victory and who Jesus is
For the unknowing to know and win

If someone tries to get the best of you
They will see by your actions that can't happen
The bond between Christ and you
is His miracle between you two

Use the best of you to serve Him
Make Him relevant in all you do
That many will see how important
That Christ has become to you

Out of Alignment

Getting an alignment is for our cars
To keep them steering straight
How many times have we steered wrong
Out of alignment with God and His Son

His word will keep us steering straight
Out of alignment will be corrected soon
Jesus is always watching our alignment
So that we'll be ready for His assignment

Jesus wants His saints to be straight shooters
Straight shooters that will hit their mark
Not too little or too much one way or another
But perfectly aimed to hit the heart

Attention to Jesus is our heart prayer
And for all people to be aware
Jesus is aiming for a heart shot
His love for you will hit the spot

Nothing no how no one will ever do
What our Savior on the cross did for you
He was all in from the beginning
To align you with your ending

To drive to Heaven's gates guiltless
Even though you came with sins countless
They were thrown out before you even got there
Christ's blood has aligned you by His care

We can never be in perfect alignment
The only perfectly aligned was He
Aligned with the Father to make a difference
For mankind to choose Jesus for our preference

Our preference to keep our alignment on track
Checking that our alignment is right
And when we are brought before Him
Are aligned with our Almighty tighter than tight

There's More to Be Had

Being uplifted by our King every day
New experiences we daily encounter
Experiences amazing to make us glad
Guess what? There's more to be had

It's like a magnet pulling us in
To a life we've never known
Being excited about what's new today
Another life for Jesus has been had

We don't know what we've said and done
Will have the hopeful God effect
To cause the people we've engaged
To give their whole heart to our King

Another and another and another
Keep coming to be made free
When we think we've done all we can
Guess what? There's more to be had

The doors of heaven are opened wide
For God's saints to come and enter in
Our life's journey will come to an ending
As for another it will be just the beginning

God will continue to do His miracles
That the lost have a new beginning
And for them to pass on the torch
That the more to be had will be had

There will always be more to be had
Until the time of this earth's ending
We came to the good from the bad
We were part of the ones that were had

His Goodness Sake

I'm so excited to write about my King
About His goodness for our goodness sake
For His goodness reaches to the heavens
It's from where He was sent from

Sent from our Father because He loved us so
He sent His Son for the good of all mankind
Jesus did teach us where good comes from
It's from our Father who we can depend on

We can depend to see His goodness
Every day with His caring in our life
Revealing to us the good and evil
And the right from wrong to champion

In my being I know how good to me He's been
And I also see Jesus being in many lives
I can see the changes that are so drastic
Lives have been softened and made right

Back to being excited for and about Jesus
I have so many stories that I can tell
Often how He's intervened for me
To keep me alive, devoted and well

I should have died numerous times
When it was over I could still breathe
Looking back I felt the presence of a Holy One
Now I know God wasn't finished with me

He picked a time to influence my life
When I was alone and only Him and me
His Spirit spoke most powerfully
It's now or never for all eternity

I thank God He let me grab hold
And to never ever, never ever let go
His purposes are clearly being revealed
In writing about Jesus and His holy word

We are part of our Father's recipe
From an ain't to a saint to make
His Word and Spirit are the ingredients
The finished product is to be our allegiance

What's What and Who's Who

What's what and who's who, that is the question
Starting at Genesis and ending in Revelation
The Father to the Son, let's make man in our image
Last of Revelation, what will be this world's ending

That's a lot incorporated in God's Word
Everything you read is intended to bless
Of the history of the people behind us
To the future of the leaders we trust

Some will take the lead by our Father's choices
To step up and step out, faithful to the end
By this gift of God he or she rejoices
With God's caring design there will always be a sending

The entirety of God's Word is the what's what
The what He assuredly wants you to know
The who's who is who He's lifted up
To touch your life in order to grow

To grow in your knowledge of Jesus
That in the beginning was the Word of God
Jesus was the Word and became the Word
That from our sins we can be freed from

How powerful and mighty is our God
And all caring and loving toward you
He's reached out through His Son with love
To grab you to guide you through

Through this life of twists and turns
With so many pitfalls that cause us to fall
The many hard times we can endure
Our Jesus is right beside us after all

The after all is everyone's life history
To be included with his living Word
How He holds us ever close to Him
Wanting us with Him forever more

So the who's who is who Jesus is
The whole world will soon recognize Him
Every knee shall bow and tongue confess
Jesus is the who's who for all to profess

I Still Will: Song of Job

There's a life lesson we all need to comprehend
Our God will always get adoration and praise
All our remaining days to the very end
Of our earthly days before our heavenly raise

We'll be raised and lifted up
As Job was for his redemption
After suffering unending without exemption
That God would be magnified and glorified

Compared to the suffering of Christ
Job had his share of lowly misery
Steadfastness and loyalty remained
From our God He would not turn away

The Lord giveth and the Lord taketh away
Has anyone been closer to our God
To accept what He gives and takes away
No matter what and no matter when called

"I still will," answered Job
When asked would he still praise his God
For who am I but a lowly one
And my God is the lover of my soul

Job was laser-focused in
To the One he would ultimately lean on
For the comfort he could gather
And say, "I still will honor You"

How many mournful days
Would Job be able to endure
From losing everything and much more
But He would not lose his righteous God

Our brother Job surely is our example
To follow whenever bad times are here
Holding dearly and securely his God ground
Even though he experienced and felt fear

Job found the light at the end of the tunnel
After enduring what only he could endure
The Father loved him and greatly blessed him
Making him a shining beacon we should be seeking

Job's song transitions from a mournful ballad
To a triumphant song of victory
He is a shining light for us
And lasting encouragement for our memory

I still will honor You!

Good for Nothing

If you are not good for something
Then you must be good for nothing
But that's not what God has for you
He's blessed and empowered us in what to do

To go into all the earth and show His worth
Being the miracle of His love by your new birth
A new creation by His intervention you have become
An ambassador for Christ and not just the some of some

If you can turn on your thoughts of Christ
Of His presence in you to make you right
To even do mightier things than He has done
And fulfill His wishes and His victories won

Christ has done the groundwork of what it takes
For us to be followers of His examples shown
In His Word the power of what He can make
Our transition to show how we have grown

From good for nothing to great for something
To bring great joy to God's angels above
One sinner has chosen to give their life
Given to Christ because of His sacrifice

Another lost soul that now is found
Proclaiming Christ and Him alone
Is who we need and all we need
To help us be the servant He wants us to be

How God can take a negative
And turn it into something good
From good for nothing to great for something
God has transformed us I never thought He would

His desire is for all of us to be
Engulfed in His presence for our lives
He wants for us to make a difference
To the people that seem so indifferent

So if someone says you are good for nothing
Consider them and where they're coming from
They are caught up in the world and themselves
It's not too late to heaven for them to come

Not Too Late to Relate

Jesus is wanting a relationship with you
He accomplished that with what He has done
He foreknew the suffering and the berating
Letting you know it's not too late for relating

Relating to Him will give you access
To His protection and His guiding
His all-encompassing love overwhelming
To forever secure you to Himself

Be joyful you're considered by Him
To be His forever jewel and gem
The person Christ has set His eyes on
Adopting you; not from anything you've done

By His grace and mercy and joy
For you to have now and forever more
When lostness and darkness was your fate
Praise God for you it was not too late

To relate to Jesus for what He has done
He calls it even for what you owed
All your sins forgiven and wiped away
By His seeds for you that were sown

Who knows from what was in your past
From a person or event that took place
And a seed was planted for your soul
Your life given for Jesus to have control

Thank God it was not too late to relate
For all of what Jesus has done for me
Now I've been released my sins have ceased
I know my freedom wasn't free

Your price You paid for me to relate
How much closer You want me to come
All the way to where You are
Leaving the darkness I have come from

You are the light that shines so bright
To draw all the lost unto You
My eyes were blinded but now I see
Able to see how much You've done for me

I've moved on from relating from my past
Pointing to the future of fallen man
How You embrace all of us nobodies
Completing Your miracles time and again

There is a time You bring us home
Our adoption by You has become complete
Now I am a child of God
A saint and someone You can depend on

And we are related to our loving Lord
Being entrusted with His great commandment
Love one another as I have loved you
And be as one in your devoted fellowship

So When All Is Said and Done

We're about to go on an adventure
An adventure of gladness and sadness
Glad for the sheep of the narrow gate
And sad for the sheep that don't follow

This is a poem so hard to write
I'll be tearing up as I go on
Thinking of loved ones not to come
To God's loving home that's just for some

When all is said and done is said and done
It will be momentous and sobering to all
There will be no more reaching out
To rescue all mankind from the fall

Christ paid the cost for the lost
There's nothing more He could have done
He's waiting for the light to go on
For all those who would come, to come

When the door is shut it will be unspeakable
And Heaven's gates will be unreachable
His Word describes how the world will be
Nothing like anyone could have imagined

There will be a horror upon the earth
It will be nothing like nothing of the past
And this will be the beginning of sorrows
No more hope of better tomorrows

If you are sucking air and reading this
It's not too late for you to relate
To the sufferings of Christ for you
All you have to do is give in and come in

The contrast of good and evil
I pray the power of this poem will have
To steer you toward my Jesus
He's the only one with the power to save

To save you from what you don't want to find out
Pointing toward the life you can't live without
Read God's word of the end of this world
Let the fear guide you to new life

A new life at a better place
And a far better greater tomorrow
My prayer is for the human race
Will give in to Jesus and follow

Follow Him to a place prepared for you
A place prepared because of His love for you
Jesus knowing His unending love
Will draw you to His amazing grace

God is amazing in amazing ways
He will discreetly make you aware of Him
Know He is and is reaching out to you
For you to be humbled by His amazing love

He wants you to want Him for a better end!

Not as Good as I Should

Being a servant of Jesus Christ our King
And guided by the Holy Spirit within us
The question arises have we done all we could
To lead lost souls to Christ as we should

Reading about the commandments
In the living Word of God
Helps us to see our shortfalls
We should not dwell too long on

If we are pricked in our hearts
From the Holy Spirit relayed by the Father
It's high time to get up and at it
Our mindset should be not to falter

God has picked us and gifted us
To accomplish His will in all the earth
Keeping our chins up as we trudge along
The final result is: God's will, will be done

Being with Jesus, He'll ask us
Have we done all for Him we can
Have you done it for the least of these
Then you will have done it unto me

There are the lost sheep looking for a shepherd
With a strong hand leading to green pastures
The green pastures are peace and loving care
It's for all people that are everywhere

Christ has passed the torch to us
To bring the lost sheep for Him to keep
Affect a life for the good of Christ
For Him to be lifted higher

When we strive to serve our King
It's not in and of ourselves
There is the Helper we are gifted with
And our striving becomes our wish

Wishing to touch lives in a better way
Better than not as good as I should
The Trinity will help our achievements
To be as good as we could

Whatever It Takes

When we think about a loved one
That steers away and leaves the fold
We come before the Lord to make
Our requests to do whatever it takes

Our great God and loving Savior
Has all the whatever it takes
He can take whatever at His disposal
Turning a life around after our prayer proposal

What we propose is what God proposes
To follow and love Him more than any other
We need to get our ducks in a row
With priorities fixed, answered prayers will flow

When we pray for others not to be left
At times we fail to remember ourselves
To do whatever it takes for us
Being yielded to our God who is just

Just to use the whatever it takes
To keep His sheep always close to Him
No one cares more for us than God
His many promises delivered on

Seeing from a distance our Lord at work
Doing the whatever it takes
Lives transformed that come on board
Another mystery and miracle You make

It's a mystery You can love so many
Christ's prayer that He would not lose any
Sometimes harsh for using whatever it takes
Glorifying our Savior for His goodness sake

It's natural not to accept whatever it takes
It's hard even to contemplate
The final outcome is your soul won for Christ
We live the victory by Jesus's sacrifice

Analysis Paralysis

The analysis of our future success
Starts early as our life blossoms
Some want to be a this or that
Wished for the adventures that follow

Before too long we're caught up in life
Doing what we have to do when we have to do it
Our lives have been steered this way and that
We're in a maze seeing if we come out

If we had any dreams they're hard to hold
Realizing everything has to fall into place
The wishes we have are almost unattainable
Striving to make progress in the human race

It's a race because some will win and some lose
It's critical what road we choose to go down
There are detours and roadblocks before us
And high water where we even can drown

When it comes to our life decisions
Decisions that we all must make
Do we decide for Jesus the Savior
The one that never leaves or forsakes

You've come to the most important thing
In life that sets your eternity
On the path that leads to Jesus
His death on the cross has set us free

Free to analyze who you are
And to analyze who you want to be
You have to see deep inside yourself
To avoid a case of analysis paralysis

The enemy wants to keep you paralyzed
Not using your mind to get away
From all His many schemes and scenes
That have an ill effect day after day

The more you succumb the harder it is
To pass from darkness to His glorious light
Be informed His love for you
Will keep you from the enemy's plight

Analysis paralysis is something to avoid
You get it when you fail to realize
There's a battle for your eternal soul
Choosing Jesus will get you to His home

Mysteries and Miracles

The mystery of man until You come back again
Why You created us is something to ponder
You wanted us to live with You
Instead of way down yonder

Yonder's a place we want no part of
It's for the enemies of our God and King
By Your miracle You have given us life
To be where Your angels sing

Hallelujah, glory to our Christ that is given
To be victorious in all our battles
Battling for our very eternal lives
Assuredly all You do for us is love driven

It's a mystery and a miracle
You would love the lowly such as us
We can't understand but are grateful for you
Your invitation to your Father's throne

The mystery and the miracles
Of all that is in Your Word
How can this mortal mind you gave
Comprehend the greatness of Your works

From being born of your blessed mother Mary
Having not known a man it was in Your plan
For Your Son to come and not to tarry
Instructions from You to do what He can

It was enough and He hit the ground running
In three years Your will was done
Forever lives would be changed for You
Your will was done by the sacrifice of Your Son

All the mysteries and the miracles
That Christ let His disciples share
Would be passed on and never die
Shared with all mankind everywhere

Christ's command for us to go into the world
We wonder how that can come to pass
He's the giver of the gifts it takes
To win souls for Christ is the task

The mysteries and the miracles
To where there is no end in sight
Are freely given by our King
We can count on Him to hold us tight

Not to be shaken or discouraged
By whatever life may bring
We have the mysteries and the miracles
Giving all credit and glory to our King

More in Store

Can there ever be a limit on us
Of God's blessings, His gifts and love
Nothing for Him is too hard a task
He knows what we need before we ask

Our God is a God of abundance
He's created everything we need
Everywhere is the beauty of His creation
It's here, there and everywhere we see

From the mountains that leave us breathless
To the sunrises and sunsets He leaves for us
For to store the memories of what we've seen
And to compare them to tomorrow's scenes

The vast beauty of His creations
The greatest painter could never capture
Having someplace to compare it with
If we are here for our Father's rapture

Will heaven be more beautiful
Than what God has created on earth
If we think we've seen all His created beauty
There will be more in store for sure

There is no bottom to His barrels
That God has to choose from
They are limitless and overflowing
His grace and giving is always showing

To give to us what we need to have
To be effective as His servants
That we can give the gifts He gave to us
Passing them along in God's love current

It's a current that blesses all
Carrying us to our Savior's call
Come to Me ye weary and heavy laden
I'll give you rest, I saved you from the fall

His love current has us moving along
Gathering the driftwood along the way
We all have been the driftwood mentioned
Heading to Jesus's driftwood convention

There's more in store before and after the convention
To do the work that has been assigned
Since we are part of the convention retention
And we have been retained by God's design

Christ has put a retainer on us
Being retained from His time on the cross
Part of His army of soldiers
Doing our part for it must not suffer loss

When thoughts of this poem's ending
Oh no, it's just the start of a new beginning
There's more of what's to be expressed
There's more in store before I rest

There's more in store in God's storehouse
For when times they will get rough
The chaos and calamity that will be here
Our Father's hand in leading will be enough

To get us to the next mountain
He will give for us to cross
Formidable as it may seem
Before long we're to our next scene

Perhaps a scene we would not put ourselves in
A scene in that God wants to be victorious
No matter how impossible it may be
It's finality for our God will be glorious

His Word and Spirit are what we need
To accomplish victory at many roadblocks
Another road opened to someone's location
Remember the clock's ticking, we're on the clock

Hold On

Hold on, Christ is coming to hold you up
From all the negatives that befall us
You get to where you want to just give up
Don't give up and don't give in is His command

Christ is right around the corner for us
He wants us to meet Him face to face
What a beautiful sight we'll see
You'll know He's here for even me

In 1 Peter 5, verse 7 it reads
Cast all you cares on Christ
For He surely cares for you
He will do what it takes to get you through

Through another day you didn't think would happen
But Christ stepped in just in time
And made His presence known
Thanksgiving and praise to Him should be our tone

Life events can wear us down to a frazzle
Day after day pummeling us down to our last straw
Remember Jesus is the creator of those last straws
He never runs out and will give you another

Christ is glorified in the last straw he supplies
He appreciates us acknowledging Him in our lives
Without Him we are nothing and with Him everything
We get to experience the everythings that life can bring

To rise above the turmoil that we often daily see
He's our faithful comforter so get close as can be
We have an expectation of what our future holds
Of Christ caring for us forever, the sheep of His fold

There can be nothing that Christ won't supply
Of whatever the needs we need we'll have
From now through eternity on Him we can rely
How You always supply our last straws

When we look back at all our last straws
We may need to name them forever last straws
We never run out of Christ reaching out
And He calls us friends and takes us in

Eternity Dwellers

The very thought of is there something after this
All mankind wonders is this question a hit or miss
It is a hit and it has hit us right between the eyes
Thanks be to God He answers, not for us to surmise

His Word is clear and concise about our eternity
God has simplified it down for us to understand
Some of us know the two choices, it's either heaven or it
    is hell
Others answer, "I don't know where we are going to dwell"

We will be dwellers somewhere after "the after this"
God has prepared a mansion for who will follow Him
Jesus will be our judge to judge us and welcome us in
Into the glories of heaven so hard to comprehend

The "I don't knows" will have their answers
Of what the afterlife could possibly be
The pain and the suffering too late to dodge
Realizing this eternity is something not for me

So before it's too late for you to decide
Of the two places you want to be
Remember God sent His Son to gather many followers
So decide for yourself of the eternity you want to see

To be a follower of Christ will be my eternity
The place of the pain and the suffering is not for me
Praise the Father and the Son they have led me to choose
The beauty of heaven where I will forever be

From the Beginning

What a great, wonderful, and mysterious God we have
That from the beginning of time He chose us
His mysterious guiding has trumped everything
To get us in position to welcome us in

The probability of God choosing us
One in a quadrillion billion
Our family generations were passed by
Thousands not pointed to His side

Wide is the gate that leads away
And narrow is the gate to redemption
To bring us along and close to Him
All through our existence was His intention

Christ made a claim that we are His
And we were chosen by His decree
John 15:16 lets us know his truth
I chose you and you did not choose Me

The mysteries of God's maneuvering
To get us to where He wants us to be
We think we've made all the decisions
But in reality He's guided us to Him

Why He would choose the ones He chose
The question that causes us to be baffled
It's not our job to figure it out
Just to be thankful we're headed to His castle

The choosing of Paul seemed the most unlikely
The brunt of the New Testament was upon his shoulders
But He came through as a shining star
His travels would take him farther than far

When Christ said you will do greater things than I have
     done
Talking about so many millions would hear His word
From His followers He was leaving behind
To go and preach His word throughout the world

How His word like a wildfire did spread
The many miracles and healings that were known
The lives that were gone and then brought back
It's Christs love to the world that was shown

From the beginning and to the ending
On this rotating sphere we call home
There's such a better place we go
Such a glorious place with streets of gold

Remember we are to plant Christ's seeds
We may not know the outcome of what we do
By our obedience and service to our King
It's what counts on our account for Him

God's Enablers

Dear Father,

We stand before You in humble beginnings
Our remaining journey with You still remains
Where we go and what we do for You
Will cause a light to go on and a life will be changed

Another life changed for our loving Savior
You've enabled us to play a part
Being guided by Your Word and Spirit
Continuing to form us since we made our start

You've enabled us with our own free will
To wisely get on Your loving ship
And who You sent to reach out to us
Is your mystery sometimes revealed

Paul's conversion and his meeting with You
on the road to Damascus with the other men
You enabled Ananias for him to receive his sight
Paul going into the world to speak what is right

You always have an enabler on hand
To do Your will with Your command
How awesome and good are You dear Lord
To reach to us with Your loving hand

Whenever there is your wind that's blowing
And it's time to touch another life
You will enable one of your enablers
To touch a life and to be made right

Your angels are always waiting ready
To be Your enablers ready to be sent
To whoever Your caring sends them
To touch a life and give them Your relief

Their life's not over and is just beginning
On the path You've set out for them
The new adventure You've put them on
To be one more of Your shining gems

Enabling those chosen to be effective
In winning souls chosen by You
Another enabler is birthed
Showing the world how much You are worth

There is no end of the many You choose
We all are enablers for Your kingdom
Your kingdom come Your will be done
On earth as it is in heaven

The many ends that You tie in
Is amazing and awesome to us
Us Your children who You've tied in
Enabling one more enabler to send

Into the world another enabler going out
It's an ongoing process that has no end
Praise and glory to Your design
And to Your service we're forever assigned

Sincerely,
Your enabler and friend

Until Further Notice

To all mankind: Christ died on the cross for you
If you don't know Him yet, He's patiently waiting
For seeds sown to take root, that's His focus
Meanwhile know He wants you, until further notice

Remember He put a notice out
That none should be lost but all saved
He's done everything of what is takes
To secure you to Himself this very day

Christ will continue to put notices out
To get the Lost's undivided attention
It will be something you will surely notice
mostly His love for you He wants to be mentioned

Christ spent the same amount of time for you
On the cross as for any other
And for your father, brother, sister and mother
Everyone is included to be welcomed in

One notice Christ does share with us
Is in Matthew 24 verses 36 to 44
Speaking about time drawing to an end
Be safely in His house for time will be no more

There are many notices mentioned
For us to have our house in order
Throughout His word He emphasizes
To watch and cover all your borders

For chaos will be upon us
Multitudes blaming Christ's chosen ones
Christ will rapture His blessed children
While on earth people with their guns

We'll be secure in Christ's own House
From time on the cross He's welcomed us in
For heaven is our eternity to share
And we're gone from what has been

The place where the enemy has reigned
God's timing will bring it to an end
His justice for who have rejected His son
Has been designed and meant to offend

Watch your time and what you do with it
Let it be a gift to our loving God
To show He's more important to us
Than what mankind can ever design

Until further notice is a reference to time
There is only so much time that's left
Before God's judgment is finally here
So decide for Christ, He wants to hold you dear

Death Defiers

Talking with the men of my Sunday school class
Did they remember times when they should have died
They all raised their hands to signify
The times they should have but are alive

We all acknowledge by the grace of God
He interrupted what could have been
God wanted us alive and serving Him
Us having no part in what could have been

Christ enlivens our lives daily
To be more than what we would have been
With Him guiding and leading
We would be lost to Hell's unending

Pain the likes have never been known
On the earth from the beginning of time
Thank God we're included as your death defiers
We hold You close and call You mine

Fear not what man can do to you
It's God's work that doth strengthen us
As death defiers we will have our place
Life forever with Christ by His grace

To be witnesses for our loving King
Our lives have been given to Him
He always knows what to do for His glory
Using us as His death defiers is our story

A story of what could have been
Our story of what we do here and now
The death that this life can bring on us
Is nothing compared to our life that has no end

With our Savior He's assuring us
In His word is often, "most assuredly"
That He will never leave or forsake us
He most assuredly has made us free

Free from death and free to life
Is the path He has set us on
It's the path of being a death defier
Our God is greater than this world's liar

Harvest Time

Consider our time to be a set amount
From our beginning to our ending
Wondering what will be on our account
Of the lives for Christ we are bringing

We don't know when our Father decides to call us home
Have we touched the lives of those intended
Going to engage with whoever is on our path
Have what we've said and done kept them from God's
    wrath

Doing our part with the planting of God's seeds
Trying to be an example of Christ's example for us
Going unto the people and attending to their needs
Their greatest need is their need of needing Jesus

The fields are white unto harvest
Christ has done all the twists and turns
Turning many lost souls unto Him
From a lost poster to the time to bring them home

The saying home is where the heart is
Christ wants to win your heart for Him
Remember before you're one of the harvested
To be part of God's family you have to forgive

Our Savior forgave the sins of many
On that day right there upon the cross
How awesome You saved the lives You saved
And how marvelous is Your harvest

The many saints we'll come upon
On our entry into heaven
But for now we're still to be engaged
In the shepherding of God's chosen

The discipled will disciple on
For the harvest to be finished and complete
And when the all of what's said and done
We will be joyful of the saints we'll meet

We're to be locked and loaded
And ever ready when we are needed
To be the servant of Christ our King
At the disposal of those that are seeded

The seeds that are for God to water
Using every means available to Him
For Christ to be glorified and acclaimed
Of the precious harvest for Him brought in

De-Clutch

The many songs we sing about the battle
The battle against the enemy of our souls
A Mighty Fortress is our God we sing
Into the fortress our families we bring

To be safe and sound and secure with Christ
A promise given a promise kept by Him
Can't we make a promise and enter in
A for-life contract with Christ the King

Stand up for Jesus ye soldiers of the Cross
The enemy is right outside our door
Trying to find ways to enter in
Subtleness He uses as our world slowly dims

He is trying to get His clutches in you
But our God and King is mightier
No matter what the enemy may bring
Jesus is all we need we believe and sing

If the enemy has any influence on you
It's time to de-clutch and kick him out
God's word has made it clear to us
There's no room in our lives except Jesus

De-clutching for us has cleared the way
For the amazing that Jesus will do in us
He wants us to be a light for Him
De-clutching will accomplish that

Instead of Jesus getting His clutches in you
His sacrifice on the cross has given us His love
And greater is His love than anything
That the enemy may devise and bring

Time is the gift we can give to Christ
It's time with Him that will help us to de-clutch
To experience amazing and all forgiving
As He shows to us He means so much

You need to love Him more than anything
This world can possibly give unto you
For what He offers and has given
Can keep the enemy's clutches out of you

So it's de-clutch time to experience
For all the ugly and yuck to go away
The loving and mighty lover of our souls
Is speaking to you this very day

Twists and Turns

How many twists and turns we go through
To get to the sanctuary of heaven
When all of life's worries fade away
Not to be found in any measure

But while we're here we have someone
To pick us up and carry us on
For His desire is for us to be
With our King forever in eternity

First we have to go through trials
Part of life we have to experience
Jesus will help us out and move us along
To be with angels singing heavenly songs

Now I'm closer to my salvation
Than when I first believed
Old man time is working on me
To free me from this life to set me free

Not many twists and turns are left
There's so many that are behind
Not many more are even left
It's almost time for heaven's rail line

To get aboard the train to somewhere
It's that somewhere I want to go
Many years on the train to nowhere
Wasted miles and nothing to show

Thank You Lord for including me
To let me see You in ways so profound
For I am so unworthy of You
One of many coming to You from all around

Not serious enough to be Your saint
You've twisted and turned me around
For my life to be in service to You
To go for Your people to be found

Come to Me all ye who labor
Are heavy laden I will give you rest
You will get help and care from
The One who cares for you the best

You Left a Mark

Jesus when You came into my life
To deal with all my chaos and strife
My confidence has not been lessened in any way
In Your care for me, even though I will stray
You left a mark

It's a mark that I've been branded with
In my spirit, it's there to stay
That mark is a light that will shine
You've gifted me to call it mine
You left a mark

Your Holy Spirit directs my light
To draw lost souls unto You
When I pray for opportunities
That's exactly what You do
You left a mark

How You mark Your family
Is amazing and wondrous to see
You've called them before time began
Not a mark outward but in the inner man
You left a mark

The outward man is dying
The inner man will live on

To be with You joyfully in heaven
Or to where the fire will never lessen
You left a mark

In Your book of Revelation
In Chapter 13 for all to see
The enemy uses outward marks
To draw people away from Thee
You left a mark

You've marked Your people on the inside
It's on the inside we're drawn to You
A place of Your protection
No matter what the enemy will do
You left a mark

Greater is He that is in you
Than he that is in the world
The mark of Him who is in you
Is the mark that will lead us home
You left a mark

Can we ourselves leave a mark
With good thoughts that never perish
Of our family and brothers and sisters in Christ
A mark of thoughts we'll ever cherish
We've left a mark

And to the many that have left their mark
Have left their mark on my heart
I will lift you up daily in prayer
And let us all remain faithful warriors
You left a mark

What's in It for Me

What a statement, what a saying
"What's in it for me"
Normally that would be a selfish remark
That thought brings us to the start

The start is who Jesus really is
And the history of so long ago
From a baby to a boy to a man
Taking on the debts and sins of every clan

In Jesus going on the cross for us
To give the greatest gift "It"
Undeserving even though we are
His sacrifice on the cross has made us fit

Fit to receive His goodness to us
In the everyday living that we do
He takes care of the birds of the air
Most assuredly He'll take care of you

What our needs are and our purposes for Him
Are ever present and will be revealed
His Word will guide and His spirit lead
Being born again we are forever sealed

You move away from "What's in it for me"
To here am I Lord, what for You can I do
You've come into my life and I love You most
Everything takes a back seat to You

A mighty and loving ruler to me
Revealed in so many and marvelous ways
I know who holds my future
To be revealed in not so many days

Am I scared or am I afraid
Of what tomorrow will bring my way
You are my Shepherd and my Savior
My trust in You is what I'm willing to pay

The payment of my trust in You
Can there be any payment higher
For all mankind You died for us
To welcome us to Your heavenly cluster

A cluster of saints won by You
Against the One who will face great loss
To overturn Lions: Many; Saints: 0
The saints have made it to their heavenly loft

To be welcomed and know what welcome is
Coming to your forever home
When to Jesus your arms reach out
To be embraced by our loving Lord

Well done is what you'll hear from Him
Even though Jesus has done us well
The combination of Jesus and us
Has kept us from the caverns of hell

And so "what's in it for me"
Has been explained and discussed
Is there anything you want more
Just knock and be welcomed into heaven's door

There can be nothing greater to have
Than the love of the Father and the Son
From the cross He reached out to all
Sacrificing all to keep us from the fall

Share a lot of the "it" you have
To pass it forward to many others
When others ask "What's in it for me"
Soon we'll be calling them sisters and brothers

Better Late Than Never

To go out into eternity forever
Having no assurances of where you are heading
God's Word will be the guiding force
As time goes on to know it's precious worth

God's so real He wants You to acknowledge Him
Who He is and what He has done for you
He's loved us so much He gave His Son
When eternity arrives He's who you can go to

There's such a contrast of heaven's sweet home
Compared to the hell that's down below
To where you don't burn up but are there
All you can think of is you want to be elsewhere

There's only one elsewhere you can go
Before Jesus you'll stand to be judged
It's an elsewhere that His word describes
A glorious place of peace where everyone is loved

Hell is where everyone endures the same pain
Thoughts of those eternity dwellers; I wish it would rain
But rain is for the growth of the living
So don't ignore what God and Jesus are giving

A choice between what is good or evil
Is the free choice God has given us
Better late than never is such a good thing
God has left the door open to come in

To be the late ones is such a blessing
compared to the never ones that turn away
From a loving God and precious Savior
Wants you to decide for Jesus today

To come on board His eternity ship
He's left the gangplank down for a bigger gang
We can all sing here, here, the gang's all here
Because here is heaven we hold so dear

Better late than never is God's gift
If you have any breath left please choose
The late that makes you equal with
All the saints we ever knew

Then never that will never be ever
In the place to share Christ's love
For they have chosen the dark path
And the pain that goes with God's wrath

But the gift of God is Christ our King
Praise God for those who came late
For they are loved and appreciated
At the end they were obedient to God's mandate

Getting Weary

How often does life take its toll
To where we are worn out and weary
Circumstances have taken all my strength
Is there any hope and help from my fearing

Fearing what tomorrow may bring
It's been one bad thing after another
How many bad things can a person endure
Is there a light at the end of the tunnel

There is a light and it shines so bright
And the dark things of life are pushed out
To make room for the blessing of God
And put an end to any bouts with doubt

There is a freedom from life's weariness
It's being yielded to the directions of God
He wants us to cast all our cares upon Him
And all our weariness will seem to dim

You'll have a strength like never before
Looking back and seeing who's rescued you
Come to Me all ye weary and heavy laden
The rest you find in Me will get you through

Your trust in Me is the payment I seek
You can trust Me for you and all your family
For I have made my payment for you
It was on Calvary to set you free

From the weariness that life can bring
There's always a way to rise above it
When the weariness of life causes strife
Remember: I am the way, the truth, and the life

The life I give can conquer anything
That would dare come against you
For my Father and I have made our claim
That your life rests in our name

Our name is a firm foundation
There is nothing that can tear it down
Leave the weariness that you have known
Welcome we say to your forever home

Though still on earth your home's secured
We have done all to get you ready
As a master potter I have molded you
For all to see you've been made sure and steady

As a ship upon a stormy sea
Remember what my disciples embraced
My caring and concern for their well-being
Can even from them to you be traced

Oops, Change of Plans

When we think we have our lives planned out
We are somewhat sure of what tomorrow brings
Surprise, surprise will come to us
Our lives' plan interrupted by the King

"Oops" there's been a change of plans
From a second ago to the second that is now
Christ has claimed my life for Him
In the twinkling of an eye somehow

For I didn't have many plans
Being influenced by crazy doctrines
My life had been a maze to me
And God's plan for me is to be amazed

Amazed there has come a change of plans
To what I thought was a good idea
My ideas were selfish to a fault
God's plans are for all the clans of man

He is all-giving and I for sure am not
Not yielded enough for my Lord and King
To go out into the fields white unto harvest
For lost souls to Him to bring

It is amazing how fast lives can change
From what was good but not good enough
Jesus has a greater purpose for us
To make us His masterpieces from what was rough

A change of plans He knew is what I needed
His time on the cross was not just for me
His plans for all mankind to be included
To be His family on our new family tree

But there is an enemy waiting in the wings
Having plans spelled out in many ways
Him knowing the saying "misery loves company"
Ultimate misery for all your eternity days

Thanks be to God who loves us beyond measure
Who has poured out His love through His Son
Through all eternity He would be our treasure
And we knowing we are an undeserving one

His mercy and grace are His plans for all
Who'd come to their table and dine with them
The Father and Son and who'd heed the call
To be blessed by our Creator's greatest win

Our "oops" Christ has considered and forgiven
He's won our souls and hearts for Him
Won against the known enemy of our souls
Christ has molded us to make us whole

Sending us out into this messy world
With the word of God and His mighty Spirit
What a freedom and we've become His light
To do our best to make our world right

What Lies Ahead—
What's Left Behind

What lies ahead, what's left behind
Is a question that in part we can answer
What's left behind of the things we know
Of the good things and the bad not shown

But we cannot get redemption from Him
If indeed we don't deal with the bad
We have to accept all the bad we've done
For forgiveness comes from God's only Son

To set us free and leave behind us
Not remembered in eternity
What's left behind is gone from our minds
What God has made is a light for Him to shine

Jesus has made us a shiny object
We are the object of His great love
To go into the world and accomplish
His will of shining for Him

We are to let our light shine for Him
It's a light that's supernatural to us
A gift from our Savior so undeserved
In order for the world to change, it's a must

What lies ahead is our equipping
The life giving light and His word
To go into the world undeterred
With the power of His might and His sword

His sword which is His word is mighty
Mighty to the bringing down of strongholds
What strongholds can stand against our King
With His will for us to leave our earthly molds

In the twinkling of an eye it's accomplished
To go from what we were to what we are
We're becoming what lies ahead for us
We're a star in God's family of stars

Well done good and faithful servant
Are the words we want to hear from Him
Not what we have done but what He has done
To make us one in Him and let us in

Into a household of Jesus believers
It's great not to worry what's outside
Nothing to do harm or injure us
I'll never leave or forsake you, on that you can rely

What lies ahead is the story of the cross
For all the world to hear and see
What was done and accomplished there that day
from many years gone by has affected me

The effect of what Calvary has had
For the many that have come to Him
Had their old lives given up and new ones had
What a miracle to share from what we've been

The answer of what lies ahead
Will be answered when we get to heaven
Now not knowing all we'll see
Before getting to heaven; I can only imagine

There will be our Father on His throne
And our loving Shepherd next to Him
Their majesty will cause us to be undone
And of the masses we'll all be one

To praise and glorify our God and King
In one chorus magnifying them
And with the Spirit that's inside of us
To lead the worship of all men

What lies ahead we'll someday obtain
Believing that we are obtaining somehow
To be equipped for our daily lives
Being who God wants us to be right now

Always

Always I feel You close to me
Wanting more from me moving on
From where I've been and where I was
To be closer to my Savior and God's Son

Not knowing of all Your plans for me
Thoughts of peace and not of evil
You've promised me a future and a hope
Your presence assuring me a way to cope

You will never leave me or forsake me
You are always near to lead me on
Though I don't have the greatest voice
The Spirit leads me to break fourth in song

Singing is a way to bring praise to You
I'm sure You're always waiting to hear
Of our love and allegiance to Jesus our King
Even when our song's inside, to You it's clear

We always want to extol our King
Our influence to be influenced by You
And the lives You want us to touch
You were aiming for before they knew

Always wanting to expand Your family
And the many hearts that are Your targets
The more the merrier what a motto
Your word gives clear precepts to follow

Always Lord You are true to Your word
The same yesterday, today and forever
It's how You keep order and us close to You
The enemy could have no hold on us ever

Always You lead us by Your teachings
in the gospels of Matthew, Mark, Luke, and John
How blest were they to be with You
Someday we will be with You and our day will come

Blessed are those who have not seen
And by Your presence they have believed
Jesus is alive and our lives He's ready to measure
Those that follow Him will find their treasure

Always know I am my Father's Son
He so loved the world and all the people of it
Through Jesus all will find freedom and life
His sacrifices and sufferings have paid our price

Always think of Me in all your ways
And to be praying without ceasing
We will look down from our heavenly throne
Your thankfulness to Us will be pleasing

From my Father and Me and the Spirit
The Spirit I sent to dwell with you
When you need help He'll be your Helper
Always with you in all that you do

And always in all that you do
Consider you are doing all things unto Me
That your work will be credited
To your account when you stand before Me

Know that to Me you are precious
I'm always looking after you
As sheep always needing a shepherd
I'll always be there for you

I'll guide you always and lead you
Unto the path that is straight and narrow
To where the goats can't enter but the sheep only
My life's given to you to lift you up from sorrow

A love gift given of Myself
That you would love Me back to some degree
You can't give what I gave to you
For I was chosen and it had to be Me

Always I will be with you
And always you'll be with Me
I have always been and will be
The caring Shepherd taking care of thee

Freedom Fighters

As Christians we are called on
By the decree of our great God
To go out and fight in all the world
Against the enemy and get it on

Lives are being ruined and lost daily
By the influence of the evil that is here
God intervened by the giving of His Son
We're to fight with His word and Spirit to make it clear

We are on the winning team that will not fail
Our ever-present God and Savior will allow us to prevail
Against the ugly episodes we will encounter
Winning another battle and it's no wonder

God has sent us out to proclaim freedom is for all
To be free to love and give and serve
And follow Christ's example with His call
To arms all ye people risen from the fall

Stand up, stand up ye people of the cross
One little word will cause the enemy to stand down
Our Father's agenda will continue to move along
To gather souls for Christ from all around

Many will experience their freedom for the first time
It's a freedom they have never known
How precious and worth fighting for
Freedom fighters your allegiance you have shown

Our freedom comes from Christ on the cross
His campaign is worth fighting for
Obediently offering our service for Christ
Christ's command is for freedom fighters to unite

There needs to be a difference and we are different
The good different Christ wants us to be
To step up and step out for who He wants
To be included in His family tree

For evil to prevail is for good people to do nothing
That's a saying we hear in our society
Freedom fighters are to be no part of that
God's directing will cause us to do something

Compassion for others will direct our actions
What we say and do will come from the Spirit
That victory in Jesus will be our theme
We will be triumphant against all schemes

So freedom fighters you have your work cut out
It's not just a saying but what we are doing
To secure lives for Christ is our motto
As time goes on there will be those that follow

Fight on!

Too Raggedy

Just how God comes upon the scene
To recruit us when we're never ready
Making His pitch for us is the mystery
Since we consider ourselves too raggedy

To fit into God's plan for us
We know how we've been and how we are
Just why God would have any interest
He knows more than we know so far

He knows that changes are coming to us
To go from what we are and are going to be
For to serve our God and Savior
Still to me, it's a confounded mystery

Christ came from two thousand years long ago
Teaching us many lessons to get us ready
That whenever the hard times would come
He would show that He's made us sure and steady

Made us sure that what we say for Him
Coming from His Spirit and His Word
To point lives to Him and forever be
Freedom fighters with His mighty sword

We say hallelujah how He's molded us
To make us steady in all kinds of weather
Whether a storm of lashing viciousness
Coming from Satan and like no other

But our God is mightier than anything
That the enemy of our souls may even bring
For God and Christ are a mighty fortress
And will out—do all of the enemy's schemes

There will be times when we look back
To the many blessings God has given us
He's entrusted us with His precious Word
And His Spirit when times are rough

Our raggediness has been replaced
With the touch of Christ's loving hand
He's molding a beautiful and new creation
To be His new ambassadors in all the land

So if you think you're too raggedy
For Christ to consider His
His calming Spirit will overwhelm you
And lift you up to forever be with Him

Do-Over

How our God and Savior knew before time began
The many earthly deficits we'd have
God sent Jesus to fill the gaps in
And that His blood would be our healing salve

To make well a soul that is not very well
We have no chance without Jesus's touch
Still having our family's sins that are left-over
Thank You Jesus You're here for our do-over

A do-over that all the world does need
To look closer to who Jesus is
Taking this away and putting that in
And before too long, we're born again

A new creation, hallelujah to the Master Potter
In forming us to know Jesus is He who matters
From a life messed up a life that was so dire
After all of this can we be lifted any higher

Closer to our heavenly home
Is the direction that we are pointed
His grace and mercy have touched us
By His choice and love we are anointed

A do-over we've needed for so long
Just in time Jesus has made us new
To be members of His heavenly garden
He gets all the praise for what He grew

Where we'd be if Christ had not stepped in
To claim us from a world so lost
And an enemy who thought he was boss
Our lives settled in Christ, it is his loss

It is our gain, our greatest gain
That Jesus just in time did find us
We can go into all the world
By our words and actions cause a fuss

A fuss that is a good fuss
Christ has turned the world upside down
A contrast of all that is so negative
From dark to light for every town

All who would come for a do-over
He so graciously will convert
From a throwaway object no one wants
To one so precious it is beyond worth

From a lostness that has no end
To a future with your saintly friends
Could there be anything we'd want more
Just get ready, Christ has more in store

Jesus Allegiance

Can there be a stronger allegiance
Than to the God of glory and our King
But before that goal can be accomplished
All of our wants need to be relinquished

Our selfish desires need to be abandoned
This self-directed writing comes back to me
Hitting between the eyes to leave my comfort zone
There can be no comfort if I don't obey Thee

Whoever we see around us that has a need
You said, "What you have done for these you've done for Me."
Our response should be, we are willing to do
Whatever to plant a seed that's planted for You

Lord You know better what will happen
When we reach out to serve as You command
Those that are waiting to see You through us
It will be their turn someday to pass it on

It's the way Your kingdom is grown
Going into all the world by Your Spirit's sending
To gather all who'd give their whole heart
There are many looking for a new start

Aligned with the One who can take us all in
To cover every need that Christ knows we have
And Jesus knows even before we ask
It's part of His on-going every day task

You can go and look forever in this world
Trying to find the treasure that can't be found
Christ is the treasure and He's right beside you
He's all of what you need just sound the alarm

It's your alarm that you needed Him
In your days gone by from long ago
If you had received Christ and invited Him in
All your miseries would never have been

He watches over us because He cares for us
There's nothing that He can't get done
On our behalf and for our benefit
That our lives will always glorify God's Son

We need to align our lives with Christ
To accomplish Christ's will for us
An allegiance so strong that can't be broken
If we obey all that He has spoken

The Ever After

Telling the many stories to our children
Most of the endings, they lived happily ever after
But in God's Word there can be a different ending
Without Jesus a horrid ever-after ending in disaster

God's Word is clear what life with Him will be like
To see His glories and love for you to embrace
The lives of the many that didn't choose our Lord
Trying to find ways for someone to take their place

There's no one anywhere that can take their place
It's appointed for everyone to stand before Christ
Whether they have experienced being born again
Or having rejected God's gift and sacrifice

There's many warnings in God's Word to the world
What life without Jesus will be like
There will be weeping and gnashing of teeth for some
Too late for the wide-gaters to have a different outcome

The narrow-gaters will be welcomed in
To God's glorious mansion in Heaven land
A room has been prepared for God's children
Warm and welcoming for their forever plan

The rich man and Lazarus in Luke 16:19
They both died and went to where they would go
The rich man to the fires of hell
Never had he seen anything more frightening

The beggar carried to the bosom of Abraham
The rich man could see the distance that does
Separate Lazarus from Him, the gulf that was fixed
And neither could pass from where he was

Lazarus gets to share in all the good promises
The rich man in God's predicted woes
The ever-after of each man's judgment
To either heaven or hell he goes

There is an ever-after we all will choose
Will it be to heaven by God's gift and grace
Or will it be to the hot and miserable eternity
Please choose Jesus, on the Cross He took your place

Accommodating

We want our lives to seem so right
Things fall into place, we don't lift a finger
But we're in danger from laying back
Satan waiting in the wings to take a hack

If we're not up and at 'em
The enemy's good at the hacking
Hacking away at our human weakness
Accommodating us with his sneakiness

Satan sits back and takes it in
Knowing how he can influence you
To do enough to capture your soul
Being the driver of your life and in control

The saying, "If it feels good do it"
Is our way of letting down our defenses
On the other hand what we should be doing
Is working to put up our fences

Fences are a way to keep something out
Or a way to keep something in
Satan doesn't want you to know
You can be forgiven of all your sins

Jesus was sent and came to our rescue
He is greater and will be the victor
Against all odds that we encounter
From all mishaps, whatever no matter

Christ will accept you into His family
And the things of earth will fade away
He's accommodated us from on the cross
We all look forward to a brand new day

Christ will always be our guard
A servant to all His children to be
That's exactly who we are to be for Him
Servants of the most sacred family

We are to be accommodating to all that we encounter
Not to be sneaky but from the heart
Letting everyone know they need the Lord
And will want to experience Him more and more

Accommodating can be negative or positive
Just depending on one's intent
The enemy's intent to wreak havoc
Our Savior's intent for all to repent

If your life is not going exactly as it should
There is a way that it really could
Know that Jesus is waiting in the wings
For your forever to be with the King of kings

The Turmoil of Our Times

Where have we been and are now and are going
Take the time to look over all these topics
After introspect, figure out what you should be doing
To handle the turmoil that we feel and the optics

It doesn't look good for our future ahead
God knows we're striving for insight
To know the seasons and the times upon us
Will we be here when events unfold with fright

God's Word says it will be worse than it has been
And worse than it ever will be
People are calling good bad and bad good
The coming of Jesus is what the world will see

Before Jesus comes events must take place
Many false Christs will come and deceive many
Wars and rumors of war have been for some time
Escalation of events with lawlessness and crimes

Will let us know the coming of Christ is soon
Keeping our eyes upon Christ's prize that was given
Salvation and the gift of the Holy Spirit promised
To bolster all of God's children to be astonished

Our loving Father who freely gave His Son
And is our everlasting hope and strength
To rescue His children from the worlds' woes
In times of tribulation He'll hold us close

What has become of the America we knew
Almost in the twinkling of an eye we've changed
Too many of our countrymen's love is gone
The oaths made to our country rearranged

Greed and selfishness have changed our country
Our country is unrecognizable from a short time ago
Didn't we used to be strong and indivisible
It seems too many are confused about what is sensible

All of our heroes from days gone by
Are keeping the soil of their resting places
In constant flux from turning over
Shouldn't they be able to rest in their spaces

Who will rise to our country's occasion
To say: Here am I for what is needed
Standing up for principles most sacred
The glue to hold America together is needed

Is someone needed when right and wrong meet
Too many choose wrong over what is right
Turmoil is brewing and soon will be upon us
All will be lost unless we stand to fight

Fight for the basics we call decency
To think of others as better than us
Following the teachings of our loving Lord
Dying to ourselves is a must

Taking up our cross to follow Christ
Depending on His promises in His Word
Never to leave or forsake us
Right beside us true to His form

His form to us will be glorious
And on this earth a servant to many
In heaven an angelic glorious chorus
Back on earth a hymn after the last supper

We depend on You, Lord Jesus
To come out on top after this life's fight
Fighting for what is in Your teachings
Proclaiming freedom for God's saints

We have seen events for the first time
Getting us ready for what lies ahead
Things have to get worse quicker
Before we receive our book of life sticker

You have marked us on the inside
Markings that will let our lights shine bright
We're on a path different from the world's
A path to choose what is right is right

How right is Your plan for Your children
That all who would come would come
Your grace and mercy haven't outdone You
We have become the kingdom of our God, it is done

About the Author

If you read my first book, "Come Let Us Adore Him," you'll realize I was caught off guard of what God wanted me to be a part of. I was soon on guard to do the writing I hope will make a difference in someone's life. Much of my working life was at the Fernald Nuclear Processing Facility near Cincinnati. I was a millwright for half of my career and a maintenance supervisor for my last half. That facility closed down and was the first Department of Energy site to be cleaned up. I have been advocating for the patriots that worked there for some years.

I most enjoy a quarter-acre vegetable garden I've been growing for some years. Most of what I grow goes to members of my church and to food pantries. Lately, I've noticed that "when to say when" is fast approaching. I'll have to ratchet down someday, but until then I'll rely on Philippians 4:19.

CPSIA information can be obtained
at www.ICGtesting.com
Printed in the USA
LVHW032111260121
677513LV00002B/198

9 781098 059767